Regina Noel

DEAR MOM AND DAD

Illustrated by Mathew Havran

TEACUP PRESS

To my own dear children, Simone and Charles:

If I should ever
forget what it was like,
do remind me.
Make me slow down.
Help me to remember.
Nothing is more important
than time with
those we love.

Love you both—to the moon and back.

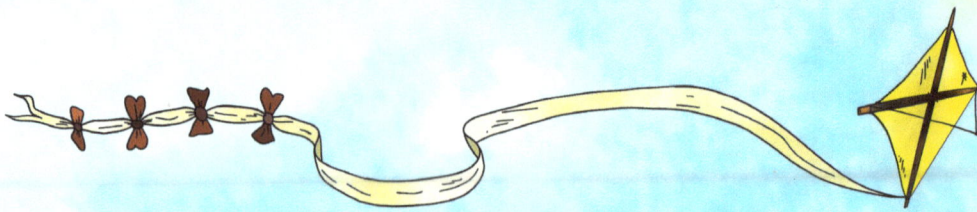

www.teacup-press.com
www.foxpointepublishing.com/author-regina-noel

Library of Congress Cataloging-in-Publication Data
Noel, Regina, author.
Eckman, Raven, editor.
Havran, Mathew, illustrator.
Farr, Chelsea, designer.

Dear Mom and Dad / Regina Noel. — First edition.

Summary: An illustrated song to help children,
parents, and caregivers communicate and connect.

ISBN 978-1-955743-53-2 (hardcover) / 978-1-952567-51-3 (softcover)
[1. Emotions & Feelings — Fiction. 2. Music — Fiction.
3. Family — Fiction. 4. Social Themes — Fiction.]

Library of Congress Control Number: 2 0 2 2 9 4 6 6 9 7

Second printing
November 2025

To Mamas, Papas, and Caregivers,

As a teacher, I am often blessed with rich conversations among my students. I am trusted with some of their deepest concerns. With the Littles, those concerns often revolve around their connection with their parents. They feel that their parents have simply forgotten what it was like to be children. That parents just "don't get it."

Our children want so much to feel connected with us, but they don't know how to say what they need. Sometimes they are just afraid to. And us parents—who can easily get distracted with the world of adulting—sometimes miss the cues.

This story songbook is meant to be a tool for families. A tool for children to help say the hard things they are afraid to say to their parents. And a reminder for parents to slow down and remember their own childhood.

Parenthood doesn't come with a handbook. But I believe so many parenting decisions can be helped by simply remembering what it was like for us when we were kids. Just like us, our kids are doing their best, too.

In a blink our children will be grown and gone. Did we miss it? The first time riding a bike without training wheels? The first band concert? The first football game? The last? The first dance? And the hard things, too, when we were most needed . . . Did we miss those? Did we forget how important those times were for us in our growing? And what about those midnight snuggles?

All our children want is to be heard, to be seen, and to be loved—and for us to remember what it was like. In the remembering, we have a newfound connection, and a newfound sense of urgency. We all know that yesterday is gone, and tomorrow is not a guarantee. Right here, right now, is all we have.

As you care for your charges, may you never forget your own childhood. There are no second chances at being a child. But as we raise them, we are blessed with real opportunities to heal ourselves.

Be present. Remember. The gift of your presence will offer lasting memories and feelings of love and acceptance to those in your care. That moves mountains.

Here's to you, doing the best you can each and every day.

Dear Mom and Dad,

please don't forget
what it's like

to

be

a

kid.

There's so much
I'd like to share
with you.

3

I fear with the years you've forgotten a thing or two.

So listen to
this song,
or maybe
sing along.

Here's what
I wanna say
to you:

School is really hard. I know I've got to think.

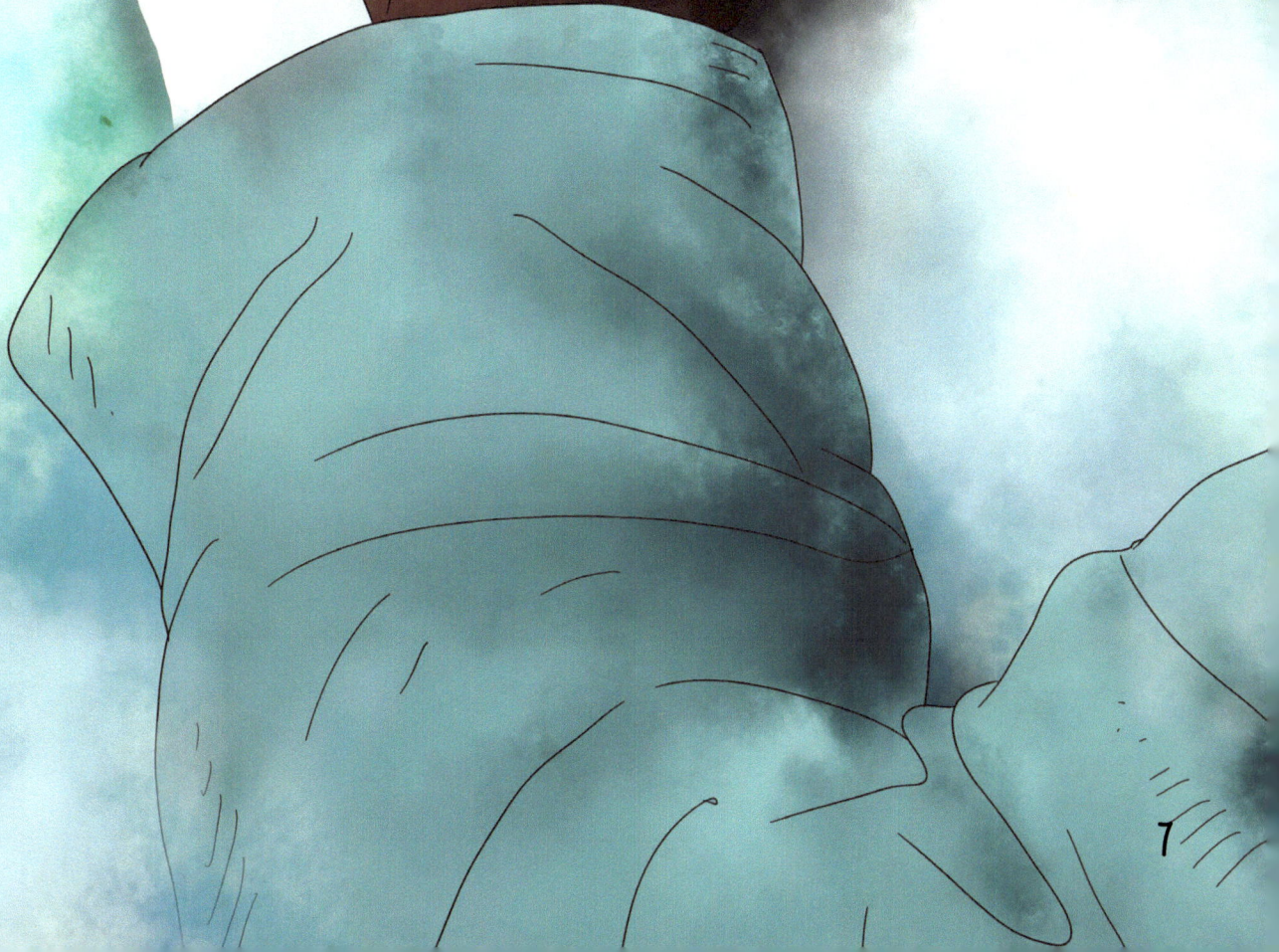

And learn a thing or two

about why the sky is blue.

But sometimes all I wanna do
is visit with a friend or two.

Dear Mom and Dad, here's what I wanna say to you:

Sometimes I don't know just what I need to do to finish up a task.

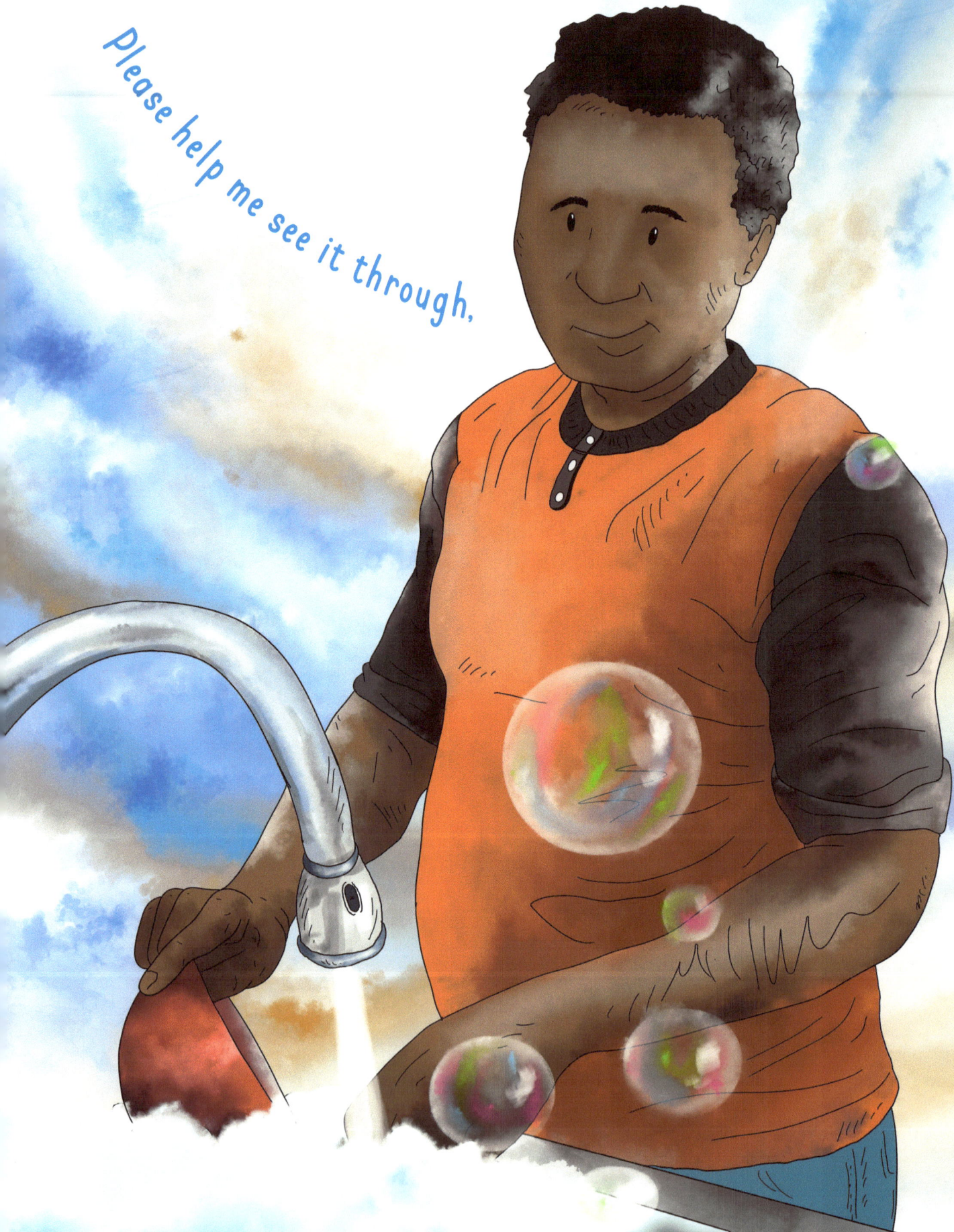

Please help me see it through,

and know that I am doing

my very best for you.

13

Dear Mom and Dad,

Here's what I
wanna say to you:
When I'm feeling mad,
I really like my space.

But after a little while
I really need your warm embrace,

16

to know that I am
loved and safe
and seen.

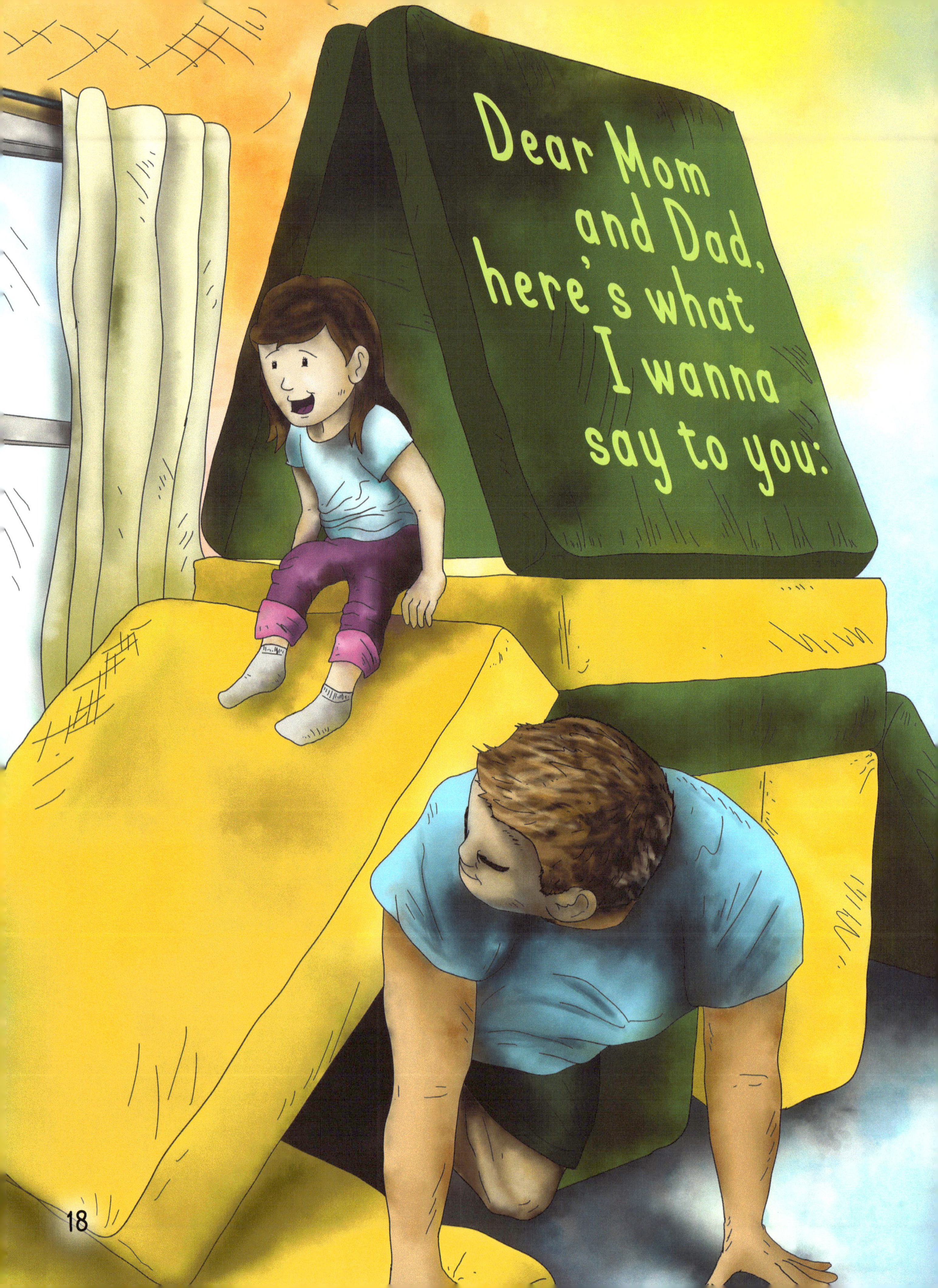
Dear Mom
and Dad,
here's what
I wanna
say to you:

Always have some fun. I know your work is hard.

But when the day is through, I really wanna play with you.

Know that
I am learning
how to live and
love from you.

21

Dear Mom and Dad, please don't forget what it's like to be a kid.

There's so much
I'd like to share
with you.

I hope with my years

you'll remember
a thing
or two.

24

So won't you **sing along** or help me **write our own song.**

25

A song about moments we'll share.

PLAY ALONG!

C

F

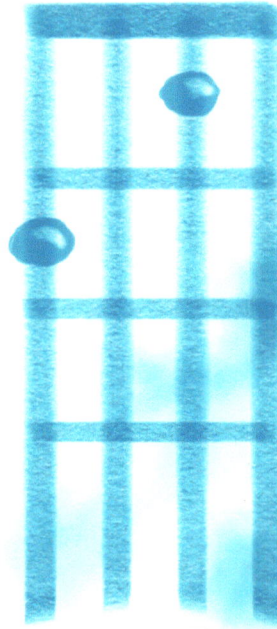

G

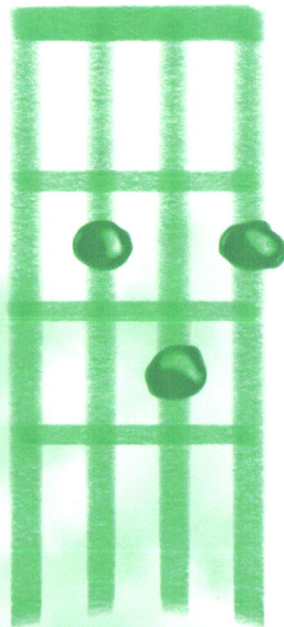

G⁷

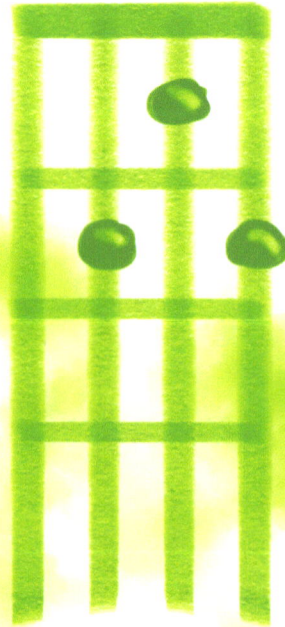

(Ukulele chords)

Dear Mom and Dad

Regina Noel

Dear Mom and Dad, please don't for-get what it's like to be a

kid. _____ There's so much I'd like to share with you. _____ *(last time)* I

fear with the years you've for-got-ten a thing or two. So lis-ten to this song, or
hope with my years you'll re-mem-ber a thing or two. So won't you sing a-long, or

may-be sing a-long. Here's what I wan-na say to you:
help me write our own ___ song, a song a-bout mo-ments we'll share.

School is real-ly hard. I know I've got to think, And
Some-times I don't know just what I need to do to
When I'm feel-ing mad, I real-ly like my space. But
Al-ways have some fun. I know your work is hard. But

learn a thing or ___ two a-bout ___ why the sky is blue. But
fin-ish up a ___ task. Please help me see it through. And
af-ter a lit-tle while ___ I real-ly need your warm em-brace, to
when the day is ___ through, I real-ly wan-na play with you.

some-times all I wan-na do is vi-sit with a friend or
know ___ that I am do-ing my ve-ry best for ___
know ___ that I am loved _____ and ___ safe and ___
Know ___ that I am learn-ing how to live and love from ___

two. Dear Mom and Dad, Here's what I wan-na say to you:
you.
seen. ©
you. D.C. al Fine

Meet the Creators...

About The Author

Regina Noel

Regina Noel resides in Iowa with her two children and two dogs. She holds a BA in Music and Physical Education from Luther College, as well as an MA in Elementary Education from Grand Canyon University. Ms. Regina is the owner and instructor of the Regina Noel Music Studio, where she teaches private piano, voice, and ukulele lessons to children and adults of all ages and abilities. When she isn't teaching or writing, you can find Ms. Regina weight lifting, making music, making (and eating) chocolates, or just plain hanging out with her kiddos and doggos.

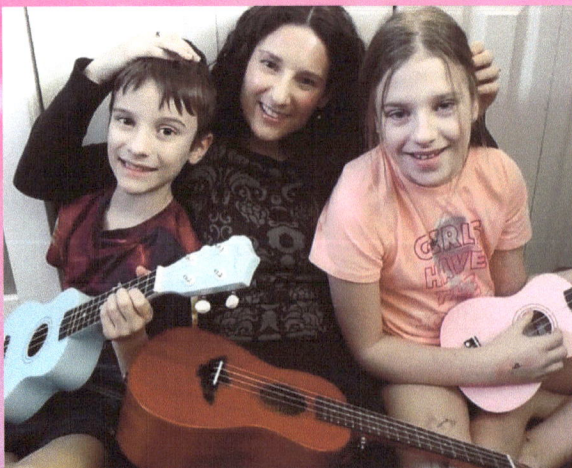

About The Illustrator

Mathew Havran

Mathew Havran of Marion, Iowa is fairly new to the world of illustrating children's books, but not to drawing and painting. A self-taught artist since kindergarten, drawing quickly became his favorite pastime up into the present. Today, some of his other hobbies include playing the piano and ukulele, rollerblading, singing and beatboxing, and family-fun activities with his wife and two kids. He currently makes a living as a Lab Technician at Collins Aerospace but has been devoting much of his free time to illustrating, painting, and muraling in his community. Much of his work can be seen around Decorah and on his Facebook page, "Artist Mathew Havran."

www.ingramcontent.com/pod-product-compliance
Lightning Source LLC
Chambersburg PA
CBHW061145030426
42335CB00002B/109